The story of the world's first
National Athletics Championships

Peter Radford

An England Athletics Publication
2016

England Athletics Publications
Athletics House
Alexander Stadium
Walsall Road
Perry Barr
Birmingham, B42 2BE
United Kingdom

ISBN: 978-0-904612-23-3

Copyright © Peter Radford, 2016

First published, 2016

All rights reserved. No part of this publication may be reproduced, stored electronically or in a retrieval system, or transmitted in any form or by any means, electronic, mechanical, photocopying, recording or otherwise, without prior permission from the copyright holder.

Acknowledgments

This has been a collaborative project involving the Amateur Athletic Association (AAA), England Athletics (EA), and the National Union of Track Statisticians (NUTS), and I wish to thank all involved for their support. I am particularly grateful to Chris Carter (AAA Chairman) who was the first to take up the challenge of this project, and for his persistence with it.

Peter Lovesey deserves a very special mention. He knows far more about this period of athletics and those who took part in it than anyone else, and he generously made available to me much of his own material, and kindly commented on my early drafts, thus steering me away from making glaring errors. There may, of course, be many remaining errors, but they are all mine.

Thank you also to Kevin Kelly for access to his original programme of the AAC's First Champion Meeting, and to Mel Watman for his encouragement and for his discerning eye that spotted early errors.

Peter Radford
March 2016

1866 and all that...

On Friday 23 March 1866, sixty-three athletes from thirty-two English clubs made their way to Beaufort House grounds, in Walham Green, on the border between Chelsea and Fulham in west London, and just west of what is now Chelsea Football Club, to take part in the first national championships in athletics, not only in Britain, but in the world. It was billed as the *Amateur Athletic Club – Champion Meeting*, and each athlete had to pay a one-guinea entrance fee per event (equivalent in purchasing power to £87 in 2016), and thirteen athletes entered two events, and one, entered four!

The programme was as follows –

11.30am	100 yds – Heats (1st 2 into the Final)
11.45am	120 yds High Hurdles – Heats (1st 2 into the Final)
12.00pm	7-Mile Walk
1.10pm	100 yds – FINAL
1.30pm	Putting the Weight
2.00pm	High Jump
2.20pm	Throwing the Hammer
3.00pm	Long Jump
??	Pole Jump
3.30pm	1-Mile
3.45pm	Quarter of a Mile
4.00pm	120 yds High Hurdles – FINAL
4.15pm	Half a Mile
4.30pm	4-Miles

The history of the Championship Meetings was off to a good start – the programme consisted of sprints, middle distance, hurdles, throwing, jumping events, a vaulting event, and walking event, and so the pattern for the future was set. In time the 100yds, Quarter of a Mile, Half a Mile, 1 Mile and 4-Miles, would morph into their near cousins the 100m 400m, 800m, 1500m, and 5,000m, but the High Hurdles were already set at 10 in number, and their height then, was the same as now, and the Weight became known as the Shot, and also was of the same weight as now, and was thrown from a 7ft. throwing area, as now, and in the throws and jumps, three attempts were allowed, and the best three were given three more attempts. All very familiar 150 years later. This was the foundation on which *all* future athletic championships were built, and, after the event, it was described as one of the most successful athletic gatherings ever held.

The track was 599yds 4 ins (547.83m) around, and was far from perfect and not particularly flat; one athlete put his foot in a hole in the heat of the hurdles, and at one point in the half-mile, the runners were described as being at the top of the hill. But these were early days for athletics, and the athletes had not yet become used to being pampered with perfectly flat tracks with meticulously smooth surfaces. More of a problem, was the weather.

There was a nipping cold south-west wind that blew half a gale throughout the meeting, but it did not deter nearly 3,000 people from turning up to see the event. It was not just a crowd, it was a fashionable one which included many ladies, and a there was a temporary grandstand that seated six hundred. Those in the stand paid five shillings, and the others, two shillings and six pence, (equivalent in purchasing power to £20.68, and £10.34, respectively, today). For their money, those in the stand got some protection from the biting wind . . . until the wind blew the roof off early in the proceedings. Neither the crowd or the athletes had it easy on 23 March 1866, and neither did the organisers, nor, indeed, the 25-strong *Band of the South Middlesex Volunteers* who, nevertheless, played a choice selection of music in admirable style, throughout the afternoon to entertain the crowd, and in defiance of the cold wind.

No illustration can be found of the AACs first Champion Meeting, but this event took place at Beaufort House Grounds in 1865, and gives some idea of what the occasion would have looked like.

From conception to completion, the overwhelming mood surrounding this first *Champion Meeting* was a positive one. Before the event, "the Committee of Nine" had worked hard to prepare the ground, and had raised £180 for prizes (equivalent in purchasing power to £15,000 in 2016) and so every winner was presented with a silver cup, and those in 2nd place were awarded a medal. There was no prize for third, nor even an official placing.

The publicity had been good, and there had been a good attendance, and after the meeting the treasurer was able to report a good profit from the meeting. Before the meeting was over, there was enthusiastic talk about next year's meeting - and so the pattern of annual athletic national championships began.

We can get some idea of the mood of the event by looking at the band and the music they played. It was the *Band of the South Middlesex Volunteer Rifle Corps,* led by Mr Hardy. They were the band of a local rifle corps raised by Lord Ranelagh, and Beaufort House was their headquarters, and the AAC's Champion Meeting only went ahead because the Corps agreed to give up their regular Friday rifle practice to allow the Champion Meeting to take place. The band's playlist included music by Verdi, Rossini, Gounod, Offenbach and others, and if this sounds to us like an afternoon on *Classic FM*, to those who heard it in March 1866, it would have simply sounded like the best popular music. All the above composers were still alive; these were the popular song tunes of the day, to which the band added dance tunes by local composers, Dan Godfrey, Charles Cooke, C.C. Chapman, and others.

Chapman was an amateur composer from the War Office who composed a gallop, entitled, *Velocipede*, especially for the occasion. It closed each of the band's two sets, and was their star piece; *The Sportsman* newspaper wrote that it was particularly admired, perhaps because Chapman was a local man, who was himself an athlete and had finished 2nd in the 3-Mile Walk in *Civil Service Sports* the previous year, held on the self-same ground on which the Championship Meeting was now taking place. He was a paid-up member of the *Amateur Athletic Club*, and a friend of C. Guy Pym, their secretary.

The Track

The grounds at Beaufort House had never been used for a sporting event before 1864, when it was selected at almost the last minute as a replacement venue for the first *Civil Service Athletic Sports*, and after their original choice (the *West London Cricket and Running Grounds*, at Brompton) had become unavailable. In the 16th century, Beaufort House was the site of Sir Thomas More's grand house that fronted the River Thames, but those days were long past and the old house had disappeared, the site sold off into smaller plots, one part becoming a Moravian cemetery, another a chapel, and a new Jacobean house was built on part of it, that too was eventually demolished and the house that replaced it had been turned into a (small) lunatic asylum. When Lord Ranelagh took it over to be the HQ of the new *South Middlesex Volunteer Rifle Corps* it was more or less derelict, but it was renovated and held dinners, concerts and plays to raise money for the Corps. The grounds, however, had been totally neglected and were described as a 'meadow' and the Rifle Corps used it as their regular rifle range. Their butts were in the middle of the meadow.

The total length of the Beaufort House Grounds was about 1000yds, but had a usable section that was about a quarter of a mile long and 110yds wide. In 1864, when the Civil Service were looking for an alternative venue for their first Athletic Sports, they looked at this long, thin 'meadow' behind Beaufort House and decided that it could be knocked into shape. With only three weeks to go Mr Jones, a War Office surveyor, began work measuring out an oval track one third of a mile in length - i.e., each lap was 586yds 2ft long (536.5m), and put down a layer of cinders, and rolled and watered them in. He also provided facilities for hurdles, jumps, throws and a vault. On the day the going was said to be good, and it is likely that the same track was marked out the following year (April 1865) for the Civil Service's 2nd Athletic Sports. But "with a year to settle down" it had "become solid", and was "practically level", but seven months later (in November 1865) the track was described as 607yds around, i.e., 70.5yds further, and was composed –

> chiefly of small, fine ashes mixed with earth; and, though it had been rolled and attended to, such a surface is rather liable to yield at the quick spring, though light foot, of runners, and likely to present, after a contest, the appearance of the application of the harrow, or some such agricultural implement.

So, the track that was laid out five months later for the *AAC Champion Meeting*, was probably very like this, except that in March 1866 it was described as being 599yds 4 ins around. There is no evidence that this track was ever built with footings for stability and drainage, or with curbs to define the edges and hold the whole thing together, and it seems likely that "fine ashes mixed with earth" were simply laid on top of the grass, watered and rolled in, which might explain how the track could vary in length from time to time; and there would certainly have been no time for major construction work in the spring of 1864 when the first track there was created in only three weeks. It is another reminder of the very considerable differences between the world in which the athletes competed 150 years ago and our own. The throwers were given almost no special facilities and almost certainly threw from grass. For the Long Jump, however, the turf had been removed and dug out 16 to 22ft (4.88 to 6.71m) from take-off, and filled with "soft clay" for a jumping pit. It is likely that the high jumpers and pole vaulters were given similar consideration: the image on p.14 shows a wheelbarrow alongside a pile of soil. Such landing areas had an enormous influence on technique – high jumpers and pole vaulters had to land on their feet! The Hurdles were probably run down the middle of the track, and seem to have had no cinders, so were a purely grass surface. Hurdles were fixed solidly into the ground, and so hurdlers had to be sure not to hit them – so there would be no elegant skimming over them; hitting a hurdle could have dire consequences.

By April 1865 a stand had appeared on the ground, described as a "covered gallery giving protection to the . . . sun, providing an excellent view of the proceedings", and protection from the wind and rain too one supposes, but this was only a semi-permanent structure, and the roof was not very substantial.

The First AAC Champion Meeting

11.30am: 100 yds – Heats

Heat 1

Although five men had entered and had their names on the programme, only three arrived at the starting line, so the day started with a depleted field. But it was far from uneventful. It brought together the oldest and the youngest men in the event: Anthony Wilkinson was nearly 31, whilst the Hon. Robert Villiers was only just 19.

The crowd hushed and all heads turned to watch. The starter was John G. Chambers who was to win the 7-Mile Walk later in the day: Wilkinson, in a violet singlet, was on the inside. Next to him was Prest, with Villiers next to him. Bang! and they were away together, with Prest, perhaps getting away the best, but they ran neck and neck for the first 30yds and then Prest inched ahead, but on the line it was so close the inexperienced crowd shouted "dead heat", but Maj. Hammersley, the referee, decided that Prest had won by a short foot from Wilkinson. Time, 10 3/4s.

Almost at once, however, a protest was made against Prest on the grounds that he was not a true amateur. In the spirit of the day, Prest withdrew for the protest to be heard, but the committee could not be called together with so much else going on, and it was decided that they would convene some time after the Champion Meeting was over to consider it. Prest had also entered the High Hurdles, and so his withdrawal removed him from that event too. Charles Prest was a 24 year-old Yorkshire man, and a cricketer who had played for the Gentlemen of the North when he was only 19, and for Yorkshire as a right-handed batsman. Later, he went on to play for Middlesex too, and it is likely that the appeal had something to do with payment he had (allegedy!) received in cricket. In their report, *Bell's Life* wrote that in withdrawing he had "waived his claim" to be called an amateur, but Prest wrote correcting them. No, after the protest, he did withdraw from the meeting, he wrote, but he did not waive his claim to be called an amateur.

The AAC Championship Meeting had opened in controversy, and it was four weeks before the committee met and published their decision which was that "the objection does not hold good"; and so Charles Prest was free to carry on competing as an amateur. We next get a sight of him in May at the Sheffield Sports where he easily won the 120yds race by six yards.

Prest's withdrawal, however, had an unfortunate effect. The rules of the competition stated clearly that the first and second placed runners in each heat were to run in the final. Prest had won, and had then withdrawn himself from the competition, but he had still won. Villiers was third, and so according to the rules was not eligible to run in the final. Prest had won fairly so could not be disqualified, so, only one athlete from Heat 1 progressed to the final.

100yds – Heat 1 – Result			
1. Charles H. Prest (London Athletic Club)		10¾s	Withdrew
2. Anthony J. A. Wilkinson (Anomalies Cricket Club)			Q
Hon. Robert F. C. Villiers (Barnes Football Club)			
Lieut.-Col. Wynne (Grenadier Guards)			DNS
William F. Maitland (Christ Church, Oxford)			DNS

Heat 2

Five had entered, but only four arrived at the starting line. From left to right the athletes lined up as follows – Lowther, Smith, Collett, who wore white with a black sash, and Emery, who wore a scarlet singlet. Hood was also listed by *Bell's Life*, and *The Sportsman*, even though his name wasn't on the programme, but he didn't compete anyway. At half way, Emery and Collett were running together, shoulder to shoulder, but at the line Emery won "pretty easily" by half a yard from Collett, who also qualified for the final.

100yds – Heat 2 – Result			
1. Charles G. Emery (Civil Service)		10¾s	Q
2. William Collett (London Rowing Club)			Q
James Lowther (Public Schools Club)			
Robert W. Smith (Horse Artillery)			
John S.E. Hood (Trinity College, Cambridge)			DNS

Heat 3

Six athletes were listed on the programme, but there was a significant non-starter - C. Guy Pym, who was the hon. secretary of the meeting, and of the AAC, and also a member of the organising committee; it was also said that he was not well, but with so much on his hands that day, it is hard to see how he ever expected to be free to run in the meeting as well! Curiously, there was another runner who wasn't on the programme: C.B. Connolly. They probably lined up - Colmore, in white and black, Vidal, in blue and orange, Philpott, in dark blue, Jobling, in blue and white, and Connolly, though Connolly may have taken Guy Pym's place in lane two.

It was a very close race until just before the end when Colmore pulled away and won easily by a yard from Vidal. Time - 10½s, the best of the heats.

100yds – Heat 3 – Result			
1. Thomas M. Colmore (Brasenose College, Oxford)		10½s	Q
2. Robert W. Vidal (St John's College, Oxford)			Q
3. Mark E. Jobling (Northumberland Cricket Club)			
Harry J.V. Philpott (Twickenham Rowing Club)			
Benjamin B. Connolly (Caius College, Cambridge)			
Charles Guy Pym (Civil Service)			DNS

11.45am: 120 yds High Hurdles – Heats

Heat 1

The heats of the 100 took only 15 minutes and at 11.45, the crowd turned their attention to the Hurdles that were already staked in place. It was to be 120yds with ten flights of 3ft 6in hurdles. Once again, the first two in each heat would progress to the final.

Four were entered, but because Prest had withdrawn after his heat of the 100, only three went to the starting line; they were, Morgan, who wore green, Smith, and Emery who wore scarlet again, and had run in the second heat of the 100 just 10 minutes earlier. At least he didn't need to warm up again! After the second hurdle, Morgan "rushed to the front", and won by 12 yards from Emery who was said to be running and hurdling well within himself. Smith was a yard further back.

120yds Hurdles – Heat 1 – Result

1.	David P. Morgan (Magdalen College, Oxford)	18½s	Q
2.	Charles G. Emery (Civil Service)		Q
3.	Robert W. Smith (Horse Artillery)		
	Charles H. Prest (London Athletic Club)		DNS

A 120yds High Hurdles race at Beaufort House in 1866

Heat 2

Four names were on the programme, but as in the 100yds, Wynne failed to turn up. So, the athletes lined-up as follows from left to right - Jobling, dressed in blue and white, Martin, in magenta, and Milvain, dressed in black and white. Milvain was ahead after a few strides and started to move clear of the others after the third hurdle, and "going like a deer", won easily by

2½ yards (although one report says he won by six yards, but this may have been an exaggeration). Time, 18 seconds.

120yds Hurdles – Heat 2 – Result

1. Thomas Milvain (Trinity Hall, Cambridge)	18s	Q
2. John B. Martin (Exeter College, Oxford)		Q
Mark. E. Jobling (Northumberland Cricket Club)		
Lieut.-Col. Wynne (Grenadier Guards)		DNS

Heat 3

This was the largest heat with five names on the programme, but Thompson did not start. The line-up was Tiffany, Vidal, in the now familiar blue and white of St John's College, Oxford, Haggard, in black and white, and Jackson, wearing green. Haggard and Jackson were both from Magdalen College, Oxford, which seems not to have had their own club colours. Tiffany was a strong favourite to win.

The race got off well, but Vidal fell at the fourth hurdle, and after the seventh, Vidal put his foot in a hole and nearly went down, leaving Jackson in the lead, which he held to the end, winning by a yard in 18 1/2s. Walter Pilkington also lists A. King (Magdalen College, Oxford) in this heat, but his name is not in the programme, nor is he mentioned in any of the principal newspaper reports, but his name was hand-written in a surviving programme of the day, but not in that heat, so King's involvement is still something of a mystery.

120yds Hurdles – Heat 3 – Result – Result

1. Clement W. Jackson (Magdalen Col., Oxford)	18½s	Q
2. Louis M. Tiffany (Emmanuel Col., Oxford)		Q
Robert W. Vidal (St John's College, Oxford)		
W.H. Haggard (Magdalen Col., Oxford)		
H.W. Thompson (Trinity College, Cambridge)		DNS

12.00 noon: Seven Miles Walking Race

This was the first of the straight finals and five athletes were entered, but one (Young) did not start: the walkers were McKerrell, dramatically, dressed in black and emblazoned with a skull and crossbones, Chambers, Montgomery, wearing dark blue, and Doig, wearing light blue. The walkers would have to cover nearly 20½ laps. Charles Westhall was the referee, and he, and he alone, could caution walkers if their action became unfair, but on the third such caution, the walker would be disqualified.

At the start, Doig, Chambers, and McKerrell, took the lead with Montgomery tucked in behind. Doig had a classic, much admired walking style with a long, low stride, McKerrell's style, however, was somewhat unbalanced, and less smooth, and was described as "stilty", with his left foot hitting the ground with a heavy "pat" on each stride. Chambers' action, too, was described as "not very pretty". At the beginning of the second lap, McKerrell went into the lead followed by Chambers. Montgomery dropped out, and Doig and Young brought up the rear, taking it in turns to pass each other repeatedly in what became a private battle at the back of the field. At the end of the first mile (8m 5s), Chambers led from Doig, with McKerrell, twenty yards adrift. At the second mile (16m 37), Chambers was about 12 yards ahead of Doig, with McKerrell now fifty yards behind. The order stayed the same at the end of the third mile (25m 1s), and the fourth (33m 32s). Chambers led by thirty yards. At the end of the fifth mile (42m 6s), Chambers seemed to be increasing his lead, and at the sixth mile (50m 47s) he was in the lead by 50 yards from Doig, but McKerrell was walking strongly about 15 yards behind Doig who seemed to be flagging. In the last mile, Chambers was about sixty yards ahead and uncatchable, but McKerrell, with his ungainly action, began to catch up Doig. Amidst great cheers, he caught him with about 300 yards to go and beat him by about fifteen yards, but with Chambers some sixty yards ahead, and apparently in no distress whatsoever.

Walking Race at Beaufort House in 1866

It was a dominant win for an outstanding athlete who had acquired his endurance as a rower at Cambridge, and who was to have, perhaps, a greater influence on 19th century sport than any other man, being a member of the organising committee of this, the first Champion Meeting, wrote the rules for boxing, which became known as the *Marquess of Queensberry Rules*, and much more. He was also the starter at this the first Champion meeting, so someone else had to be drafted in to start the 7-Mile Walk, though, as it turned out Chambers could probably have started it and then joined in and still won with ease!

Chambers was listed in the programme as competing for the Public Schools Club, but he had only recently graduated from Trinity College, Cambridge, so this event was a triumph for

Cambridge who took all three places, and for Trinity College in particular whose athletes were first and second.

7-Miles Walk – Final – Result

1. John G. Chambers (Public Schools Club)   59m 32s
2. Robert M. McKerrell (Trinity College, Cambridge)
3. William Doig (St. John's College, Oxford)
   Hugh de Fellenbuerg Montgomery (Christ Church, Oxford)   DNF
   Lt. F. Young (2nd Life Guards)   DNS

1.10pm: 100 yds – Final

With Prest's withdrawal there were only five runners in the final. The most well known was probably Anthony Wilkinson who was a well known cricketer from Co. Durham, and who had played for the Gentlemen vs. the Players, and who would go on to play in over 60 First-Class matches, but Thomas Colmore (21) was probably the favourite, having won the fastest heat.

The athletes who lined up were, Wilkinson, Emery, Collett, Colmore, and Vidal, but in what order is not known. It was a good start and close all the way, and described as a "desperate struggle", and full of incident. There were no lanes, and strings between the lanes had not yet been adopted, so in a close race it was quite possible for athletes to get in each other's way. Part way through the race Emery and Colmore collided, but it is always difficult to apportion blame in such circumstances; one report said that Emery "cannoned against" Colmore, and another wrote that Emery was the one who was cannoned against. Whoever did the cannoning, Emery came off the worst and was "completely put out of his stride", and Colmore won by about six inches from Vidal, who was either a foot or half a yard ahead of Collett depending on whose report you believe. Colmore's time was 10¼s, much the fastest time of the day. Only the first three were officially placed.

100 Yards – Final – Result

1. Thomas M. Colmore (Brasenose College, Oxford)   10¼s
2. Robert W. Vidal (St John's College, Oxford)
3. William Collett (London Rowing Club)
   Charles G. Emery (Civil Service)
   Anthony J. A. Wilkinson (Anomalies Cricket Club)

1.30pm: Putting the Weight 16lbs

One interesting feature of the timetable was that field events did not go on simultaneously with track events, so, at 1.30, after the excitement of the 100 yards final, all the crowd turned their attention to the excitement of Putting the Weight. There were three competitors, but Cheston did not compete, so Fraser, dressed in grey and blue, competed against Elliott, dressed in light blue. Almost at once, however, there was a protest against Fraser's amateur status, based, it seems, on his having practiced with professionals at the Agricultural Hall.

A Putting the Weight/Shot competition at Beaufort House in 1866

Captain Charles Fraser was cast in a completely different mould from Charles Prest, however. He was a Scot from Glenlivet, who had gone to London and joined the Metropolitan Police in 1858, and so was a policeman of some 8 years experience, and when the objection to his status was raised he ridiculed it, and ignored it. Everyone else seems to have followed suit, for Fraser continued in the competition, and the AAC Committee never considered the protest, or made any further comment on it. Despite being in the police, Charles Fraser competed as "*Captain Fraser*", *unattached*. The title "Captain" may have been from his involvement in the Volunteers. As a thrower, however, Captain Fraser seems to have been an almost unknown entity and surprised almost everyone when he won with a throw of 34 ft 10 ins, which was described as "extraordinary". Some reports claim that the shot was not 16lbs, but was 18lbs 10ozs. Sometimes *Putting the Weight* was called *Putting the Shot*.

Putting the Weight 16lbs – Final – Result	
1. Captain Charles G.L. Fraser (unattached)	34ft 10ins.
2. George Elliot (Trinity College Cambridge)	30ft 4 ins.
C.C. Cheston (Merton College, Oxford)	DNS

2.00pm: High Jump

Four athletes had entered the event and all turned up. They were Smith, who had already competed in the heats of the 100yds and 120yds Hurdles, Little, dressed in dark blue and white, Green, wearing red, black, and blue, and Roupell, wearing black and white. The rules required that the competitors had to agree among themselves the height at which the bar was first set. They agreed on 4ft 8ins. All cleared, and the bar was systematically raised with everyone clearing it, until 5ft 6ins, at which height Smith was eliminated. Green went out at 5ft 7ins. leaving Little and Roupell to battle it out. Little failed twice at 5ft 7ins but cleared it on his third attempt. At 5ft 8ins, Little cleared it on his first attempt, but Roupell failed, but "flew over it" on his second attempt. The bar was then set at 5ft 9ins, and Roupel cleared it, followed by Little. At 5ft 10ins, however, both failed, and as there was no count-back rule that took into account the number of jumps or failures, the competition was declared a tie with both clearing 5ft 9ins.

A High Jump competition at Beaufort House in 1866

High Jump – Final – Result

1=	Thomas G. Little (Peterhouse College, Cambridge)	5ft 9ins.
1=	John H.T. Roupell (Trinity Hall, Cambridge)	5ft 9ins
	Charles E. Green (Trinity College, Cambridge)	5ft 7ins
	Robert W. Smith (Horse Artillery)	5ft. 6ins

2.20pm: Throwing the Hammer 16lbs

By this time, the cold easterly wind had picked up, and blew directly in the faces of the throwers. Four had entered and all turned up. They were Fraser, who had earlier won the Putting the Weight event, Moffatt, who wore white with blue stripes, Morgan, who had previously run in the final of the 120yds Hurdles, and James, who wore red and black. The wind seems to have particularly hampered the throwers, but after "a sharp contest", James came out the winner.

Throwing the 16lb Hammer at Beaufort House in 1866

Throwing the Hammer, 16lbs – Final – Result

1.	Richard .J. James (Jesus College, Cambridge)	78ft 4ins.
2.	David P. Morgan (Magdalen College, Oxford)	75ft
	Douglas Moffat (Christ Church, Oxford)	
	Capt. Charles G.L. Fraser (unattached)	

3.00pm: Broad Jump

Six athletes were listed in the programme, but Lowe, and Maitland did not take part. These were early days for athletics and the nomenclature had not yet settled down. The programme listed the event as the *Broad Jump*, and most of the newspapers that reported it followed their example, but *The Sportsman*, called it the *Long Jump* from the outset. The four athletes who contested the event were, Fitzherbert, who wore red, black and blue, Smith, who must have been a favourite of the crowd having already competed unsuccessfully in the 100yds, 120yds

Hurdles, and High Jump, Little, who had been the joint winner of the High Jump, and Boyle, who wore white with a red sash. At least one of the jumpers had more enthusiasm than skill or experience, and amused the crowd by "tumbling about almost every time he jumped". In the end though, Fitzherbert won with a jump of 19ft 8ins, preventing Little from becoming a double jumps winner by four inches.

Broad Jump – Final – Result	
1. Richard Fitzherbert (St. John's College, Cambridge)	19ft 8ins.
2. Thomas G. Little (Peterhouses College, Cambridge)	19ft 4ins
Robert W. Smith (Horse Artillery)	
Joseph B.S. Boyle (Temple)	
J. Lowe (Jesus College, Cambridge)	DNS
W.F. Maitland (Christ Church, Oxford)	DNS

Between 1.30 & 3.30pm: Pole Jump

The Pole Jump took place at about this time, but precisely when is not known. It did not appear on the programme or in any of the earlier lists of events when the meeting was first advertised.

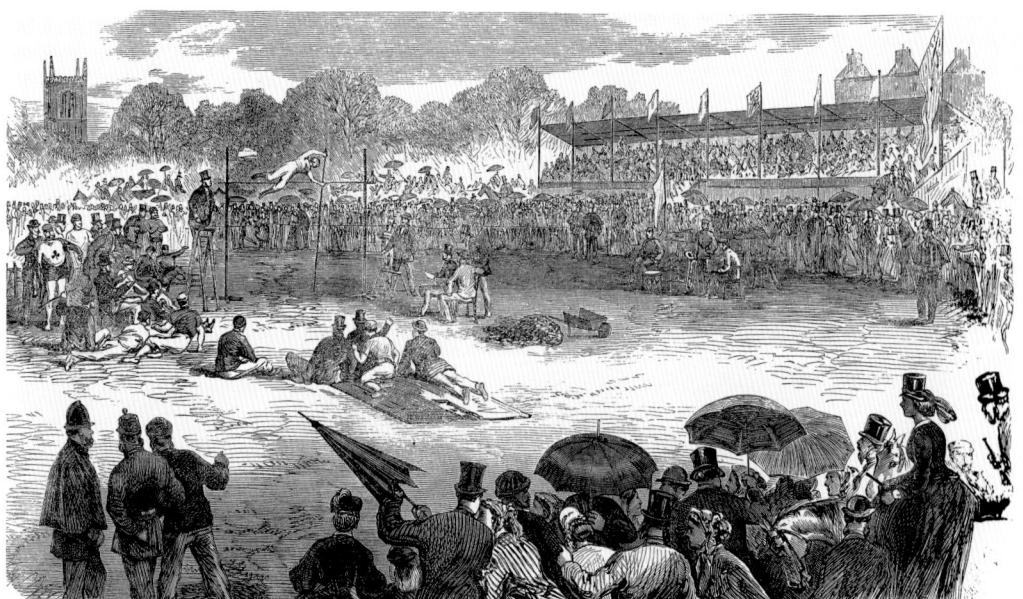

A Pole Vault competition at Beaufort House in 1866

Its first mention was on 28 February when it was included in the list of events published in newspapers about the forthcoming Champion Meeting. It was described as the *Running High Pole Jump*. However, when a list of all entries were published on 17th March, the event was still not listed and so we have no record of who entered; from the way it was reported, however, it seems to have been fitted in among the other field events before the One Mile at 3.30pm. which was made all the easier by none of the vaulters being entered in any other event. There were three of them: Wheeler, Ewbank, and Lambert. Precisely why the Pole Jump was added to the programme so late is not known. Somebody must have made a powerful case for it, and it seems likely that it was at least one, if not all of those who eventually took part. A prime candidate must be Richard Lambert; he was a senior athlete in the Civil Service and would have known C. Guy Pym well; they were both on the committee of the Civil Service Sports, and Pole Leaping was on the programme of the Civil Service Sports, and Lambert had won the event in 1864 and 1865. He was also much the oldest competitor in the meeting being nearly 39, and was senior to Guy Pym in the Civil Service too.

Lambert, however, was the first to go out being unable to go above 8ft 3ins. Ewbank went out at 10ft, which Wheeler was said to have cleared "cleverly".

Pole Jump – Final – Result

1.	F. Wheeler (Wandsworth Club)	10ft
2.	Christopher C. Ewbank (Clare College, Cambridge)	9ft 3ins
	Richard E. Lambert (Civil Service)	8ft 3ins

3.30pm: One Mile

After two hours of field events the crowd's attention was drawn back to the track. Five runners had entered, but the Earl of Jersey did not run, so Chambers lined the runners up as follows from the inside: Lawes, wearing light blue, Chinnery, wearing green and gold, Bowman, and Villiers who had already run in the 100yds. The Hon. Robert Villiers was the younger brother of the Earl of Jersey.

On the word "go", Lawes took the lead and set a good pace with Chinnery, Bowman and Villiers tucked in behind in that order. Lawes was thought to be running well within himself. At the end of the first lap, Lawes led by two yards with the others in a cluster behind. On the second lap (599 yard) the young Villiers lost contact with the others and dropped out. Lawes continued in front, extending his lead, and at the finish entered the home straight five yards in front, with Bowman who had been a poor third, beginning to catch Chinnery. This was a surprise as Chinnery was expected to do much better. There was great excitement and noise with Lawes and Bowman's fans cheering wildly, but Bowman was unable to catch Lawes who won by twelve yards. Chinnery pulled up and stopped only eight yards from the finish. Winning time, 4m 39s.

One Mile – Final – Result

1.	Charles B. Lawes (Trinity College, Cambridge)	4m 39s
2.	William P. Bowman (University College, Oxford).	
	Walter.M. Chinnery (London Athletic Club)	DNF
	Hon. Robert Villiers (Barnes Football Club)	DNF
	The Earl of Jersey (Balliol College, Oxford)	
	[Victor Child Villiers, 7th Earl of Jersey]	DNS

3.45pm: Quarter of a Mile

There were four names on the programme, but with C. Guy Pym's withdrawal (see 100 yards above), the field was reduced to three: Beardsell, who was in black and white with a blue hoop, Wilkinson, who had run in the 100yds final, and Ridley, a 17-year-old student still at Eton; he wore scarlet.

There are three different accounts of the race. In one, Ridley shoots into the lead at the start and is never headed, and in another, Ridley starts the fastest but is caught by Wilkinson at the beginning of the home straight and looked a certain winner; "Wilkinson wins", shout the crowd, but Ridley responds and beats Wilkinson in the home straight. In the third version, Wilkinson makes the early pace and leads all the way until the home straight and seemed likely to win, but Ridley "put in a tremendous spurt", and came home the winner. In all versions, Ridley wins by six yards in 55 seconds. It was a triumph of youth over experience, but Ridley was a very talented athlete and would probably have won no matter how the race had been run. He successfully defended his title the following year, when he also won the 100.

Quarter of a Mile – Final – Result

1.	John H. Ridley (Eton College)	55s
2.	Anthony J. A. Wilkinson (Anomalies Cricket Club)	
	Charles W. Beardsell (Lincoln's Inn).	
	Charles Guy Pym (Civil Service)	DNS

4.00pm: 120 yds Hurdles – Final

It had been over four hours since the hurdlers had run the heats and qualified for the final, and in that time Morgan had competed in the Hammer Throw, finishing 2nd, and Emery had run in the final of the 100. The others were fresh.

It began with a false start, the first of the Championships, but on the second attempt they were all away and took the first hurdle together, and then Tiffany began to ease ahead followed by Morgan. Morgan caught his foot in the top of the fourth hurdle and fell heavily. At the fifth, Milvain had got on equal terms with Tiffany and began to show ahead, and at the finish, he was half a yard ahead of Tiffany who aggravated an injury to his right leg sustained in the heats, and was quite lame at the finish. It was a "desperate race" between Milvain and Tiffany over the last five hurdles. Emery never got on terms with the rest and had run "somewhat tame", it was said.

120yds. Hurdles – Final – Result

1.	Thomas Milvain (Trinity Hall, Cambridge)	17¾s
2.	Louis M. Tiffany (Emmanuel Col., Oxford)	
	Clement N. Jackson (Magdalen Col., Oxford)	
	John B. Martin (Exeter College, Oxford)	
	Charles G. Emery (Civil Service)	
	David P. Morgan (Magdalen College, Oxford)	DNF

4.15pm: Half-a-Mile

Four athletes were entered on the programme and all competed. At the start they were, Thornton in light blue, Gibbs, in red and black, Collett, in white with a black sash, and Mitchell. All were fresh having run in no events earlier in the day, but all must have had a hard task keeping warm in the biting wind.

At the start Thornton dashed into an early lead, setting a fast pace in difficult conditions; Thornton described how there was "a tempest of a wind" that blew straight against them for most of the distance. The rest struggled to close the gap. At 440yds he was ten yards ahead, and "at the top of the hill"(!) Collett and Mitchell gave up the chase. Collett's problem was that someone trod on his heel and he lost a shoe. Gibbs did his best to overhaul Thornton, but to no avail. Gibbs, however, was credited with running with "the greatest of gameness", but he was outclassed. Thornton had led from start to finish, dominated every stride of the race, and won by ten yards. Time, 2m 7secs.

Half a Mile – Final – Result

1.	Percy M. Thornton (London Athletic Club)	2m 7s
2.	William C. Gibbs (Jesus College, Cambridge)	
	William Collett (London Rowing Club)	
	Edward B. Mitchell (Magdalen College, Oxford)	

4.15pm: Four Miles

The final event had the greatest number of entries. There were eleven names in the programme, but two (Beardsell and Johnson) didn't start. An additional runner (Cadman) was permitted to run, so there were ten runners who started in two rows, as follows, Garnett, in black and white with a blue hoop, Digby, wearing green and silver, Molloy, wearing mauve and black, Farran, wearing pink, and Montgomerie, and in the second row, Witty, wearing blue with black stripes, Barne, wearing pink and white, Moffatt, and Royds, in white and scarlet, and Cadman. They wore almost every colour in the rainbow, and an expectant buzz went through the crowd. It was the highlight of the day, and the crowd had stayed to see it.

It was a good start and the whole field set off in a bunch; the four miles would take about eleven and three quarters laps. When the runners settled down, Garnett was in front, followed by Farran, Cadman, Digby and Witty, in that order, but with no-one out of touch. On the second lap, Royds moved into third place, but Garnett and Farran led and increased the pace, and by the end of the first mile the field began to spread out. On the fifth lap, Barne gave up, and Cadman fell, shaking himself up badly. Throughout the race Garnett led, unchallenged, and at half way led by fifty yards. Behind him, Royds managed to pass Farran. On the ninth lap, Farran gave up, leaving the race to Garnett and Royds, who gallantly chased Garnett, but to no avail, Garnett won comfortably by fifteen yards, and the chasing Royds collapsed on crossing the line in second place. In many ways, however, Royds, the schoolboy from Eton, was the hero of the race. He was only 18 (Garnett was 23) and he ran himself out, with the crowd shouting and screaming encouragement. He looked even younger than his years and was variously described as a "lad" and a "boy", but he had shown man-like courage in chasing Garnett, even gaining on him at the end. Within minutes of collapsing, however, he was on his feet walking again and receiving even more applause from the appreciative crowd.

The splits were

Mile 1	5m 20s	
Mile 2	5m 40s	11m 00s
Mile 3	5m 27s	16m 27s
Mile 4	5m 14s	21m 41s

Garnett leading throughout.

The various reports differ in details, but everyone's attention was seized by the main performers, and how some of the lowly places fared, and even if some of them finished at all, is not always clear. The following is the best guess.

Four Miles – Final – Result

1.	Richard C. Garnett (Trinity College, Cambridge)	21m 41s
2.	Edward Royds (Eton College)	
	Bernard C. Molloy (London Rowing Club)	
	Douglas Moffatt (Christ Church, Oxford)	
	Kenelm T. Digby (London Athletic Club).	DNF
	Charles F. Farran (London Rowing Club).	DNF
	Frederick Witty (London Athletic Club).	DNF
	Capt. Frederick St.J. N. Barne (Scots Fusilier Guards)	DNF
	William J. Cadman (St Peter's College, Cambridge)	DNF
	Hon. George A. Montgomerie (Oxford)	DNS
	A.H. Johnson (Exeter College, Oxford)	DNS
	C.W. Beardsell (Lincoln's Inn)	DNS

A splendid day's sport

And so ended the first AAC Champion Meeting the first athletics national championship anywhere in the word, and the crowd went home happy. They had endured a bitterly cold gale-force wind, but they had had over five hours of entertainment, with thrills and spills galore, close competitions, unexpected results, extraordinary variety, and no small measure of controversy. But they had seen skill, and application, and even more enthusiasm in every event, and had gone home with the vision of youthful, never-say-die courage and with commitment fresh in their minds and the shouts and applause of the appreciative crowd in their ears. The whole thing had gone off on time and there was barely a lull in the whole of the five hours of action, and the band kept them entertained throughout. What a triumph. No wonder it was described as "a splendid day's sport", "an unqualified success" and that the crowd went home "highly delighted with the treatment afforded them", and that it was "one of the most successful athletic gatherings ever held".

Prize-giving after the Civil Service Athletic Sports in April 1866. Note that the roof of the grandstand has already been re-designed and repaired.

The success of the first *AAC Champion Meeting* guaranteed that there would be another and another and another. The AAC followed it up by putting on their *Champion Meeting* for the next fourteen years, all based on a mixture of sprint events, middle and long distance running, walking, hurdling, throwing, jumping and a vault. Distances would be modified from time to time, events would be added or discarded (but usually added), but the basic model from March 1866 was followed, and when the AAC was dissolved in 1880 and the AAA took over the promotion and running of the Championships, under their supervision, *The AAA Championships* became one of the most important athletics meetings in the world. And then, other nations took up the idea of national athletics championships for themselves, and as the years went by, multi-national championships appeared - the Olympic Games, the European Championships, The World Championships, and of course, women took their place in the various Championships too, but the basic model of the 1866 *AAC Champion Meeting* remained

It was a very important landmark in the history of athletics, but it was not the beginning of athletics itself. Some of the events can be traced back to ancient Greece. In the modern world, the *Six Feet Club* put on a sports meeting in Edinburgh with a steeplechase, throwing, and a running event in 1827, and later in that year jumps were added in the *St Ronan's Border Club* meeting. By 1831 the boys of *Shrewsbury School* had started their regular cross-country runs, and before the end of the 1840s the *Royal Military Academy* had started its annual athletics meeting, and in 1850 *Exeter College, Oxford* had held its first Autumn Meeting of steeplechase, sprints and hurdles.

The 1860s brought a change of pace. Deerfoot (Api-Kai-ees), an American Blackfoot runner, arrived in Britain and created something of a sensation. The public saw in him the spirit of the Noble Savage, a rekindling of Rousseau's idealism about the benefits of a natural existence, and the virtues and freedom that comes with a simple life. Running with the wind in your hair and the air on your limbs became an ideal. But as with all things, major change has complicated parentage; many of the young men who were revelling in the new athleticism at Oxford, Cambridge, and in London, were rowers, and for them the air, the exercise, the simple experience of testing oneself in simple tasks, required a contest with a worthy foe, and for that to be satisfying, they had to be fit.

In the winter of 1861/2 the members of the *West London Rowing Club* took their fitness for the forthcoming 1862 rowing season so seriously, they came up with the idea of putting on three sporting meetings to motivate their members in their winter training, and provided prizes to increase the motivation. At first, the intention seems to have been to encourage their members to do more running training, and so they put on a meeting in November with the following events - 150yds, Quarter-of-a-Mile, Half-a-Mile, and 1 Mile. Some professionals were on the ground on that first winter meeting, and a purse was subscribed so that they could race too. The meeting was deemed a success, and an even broader cross-training idea began to emerge, and in their second meeting, in January, the Long Jump was added. By February, their last winter meeting, the High Jump and a Hurdle race had been added too. In 1868, Wilkinson described the importance of these meetings in the winter of 1861/2 -

> The first spectators came to jeer, but remained to applaud, and went away very strongly possessed in favour of athletics.

In those few, short years, the athletics meeting had arrived. In 1863 *The Mincing Lane Club* was formed, and Cambridge formed a *University Athletics Association*. In March 1864 the first *Oxford v. Cambridge Athletic Sports* were held at Oxford, followed seven weeks later by the first *Civil Service Athletics Sports* at Beaufort House.

Rowers, and athletes from Oxford and Cambridge Universities, and from the Civil Service were in the vanguard of this new sporting movement, and of course were represented on the *Committee of Nine* that set up the *Amateur Athletic Club* and organised its first Champion Meeting.

The Amateur Athletic Club

The meeting that set up the *Amateur Athletic Club* was held at the *Charing Cross Hotel*, London, on 18 December 1865, it wasn't a large meeting, but we know the names of fifteen who were there, and there were apparently several others. It is not known who called the meeting, but those who gathered that day were largely men from the army, the Civil Service, Oxford and Cambridge Universities, Association Football, and rowing. Most were in their twenties and still competing, and only one of them seems to have been over forty. Those present were, J.G. Chambers, A.W.T. Daniel, Major F. Hammersley, H. Hannam, W.G. Herbert, T. Martin, E.B. Michell, J.L. Pattisson, Herbert Playford, C. Guy Pym, J. Round, P.M. Thornton, R.E. Webster, A.J. Wilkinson, and Fred Young. The group elected Major Hammersley to the chair for the night, and then set about creating a working committee of nine which would work out what had to be done to create what would become the first Governing Body in Athletics. The *Committee of Nine* were -

Colonel the Hon. H.H. Clifford

Colonel F. H. Bathurst

J.G. Chambers

Major F. Hammersley

The Earl of Jersey

C.B. Lawes

E.B. Michell

C. Guy Pym (Honorary Secretary)

R.E. Webster

It included four men who were not even present at the meeting but whose status was deemed so important they were elected anyway: they were Col. Clifford, who was 39 and was a serving army officer who was not only a holder of the *Victoria Cross* (earned at the Battle of Inkerman in 1857), but also of the *Légion d'Honneur*, and the *Order of Medjidie*, its Turkish equivalent; Colonel Frederick Hervey Bathurst, aged 32, who was an old Etonian, ex Member of Parliament, and a county cricketer from a famous cricketing family; The Earl of Jersey (Victor Albert George Child Villiers, 7th Earl of Jersey), who was 20, an old Etonian, currently at Balliol College, Oxford, a member of Barnes Football Club, and who had competed in the One-Mile (finishing 2nd), and Two-Miles (finishing 3rd) in the *Inter Varsity Athletic Sports* earlier in the year, and so was one of the young, competing athletes of the day; and Charles Bennett Lawes, who was 22, and was also an old Etonian, and a student at Trinity College, Cambridge. He had won the 1-Mile in the inaugural *Inter Varsity Athletic Sports* in 1864, and was also a very successful rower, and in April 1865 he had stroked the unsuccessful Cambridge eight in the *Inter-Varsity Boat Race*, but he had won the *Colquhoun Sculls* in 1862, and won the Diamond Challenge Sculls at the *Henley Regatta* in 1863, and the *Wingfield Sculls* in 1865, and so was another competing athlete, and an important link to the rowing world.

Major Frederick Hammersley, who took the chair at that first meeting, was 41 and probably the oldest man in the room, and was thought, by those present, to be the most suitable man to chair the proceedings by virtue of his age, his rank, and because he was the Inspector of Military Gymnasia at Aldershot. Under his leadership the first gymnasia had been built at Aldershot, at the Curragh, and at Chatham, and already in 1865 he had published the *Army Physical Training Regulations*, at which point physical training became the basis of a new recruit's life, and Major Hammersley had an interest in *The National Olympian Association* which was formed that year, and in the *Liverpool Gymnasium* opened in November.

Also among those present and elected onto the *Committee of Nine* was Richard Everard Webster. He was 23, and a student at Trinity College, Cambridge, and was one of the group of undergraduates that set up the *Cambridge University Athletics Association* in 1862. As an athlete he competed in the first *Inter Varsity Athletic Sports* in March 1864, finishing 2nd in the Steeplechase, losing by six yards. The following year he won the 1-Mile event in the same meeting by virtue of his better finish.

Another athlete elected onto the committee was Edward Blair Michell, who was 23, and a student at Magdalen College, Oxford. He was an active competitor in athletics, rowing and boxing, and was 4th in the 120yds hurdles in inaugural *Inter-Varsity Athletic Sports* in 1864.

Yet another, was John Graham Chambers, indeed, it has often been claimed that Chambers was the driving force behind the ideas that led the AAC to initiate the first *Champion Meeting*. Born in February 1843 in Llanelli into a well-known family of landowners, J.J. Chambers was sent to Eton where, by the age of sixteen he was rowing in the Eton Lower Eight against Cambridge University. But rowing wasn't his only sport at Eton, he also took part in throwing events, and was also involved with the Eton College Beagles.

In May 1861 Chambers matriculated at Cambridge University and entered Trinity College, and in his first year rowed at number two for Cambridge in the *Inter-Varsity Boat Race*, and later in the year rowed for the *Third Trinity* crew at the Royal Henley Regatta. *Third Trinity* was a club made up of those at Trinity College, Cambridge who had been at school in either Eton or Westminster. He was among the elite of the elite, and in the following year he rowed at number seven in the *Inter-Varsity Boat Race*, but as in the previous year, was on the losing side.

He went on to become President of the *Cambridge University Boat Club*, and in only his second year was invited to join the committee that reorganised Cambridge University Athletics, and two years later, the committee that set up the *Inter-Varsity Athletics Sports*, though, in both cases in a minor capacity at first. His energy and "inspiring mind" soon had an effect on his contemporaries however. He was a very successful rower and was captain and coach to the Cambridge University rowers, and through his position and status in rowing he was invited in March 1865 to become a member of the committee that organised the *Cambridge University Athletic Sports* at which he acted as starter and "discharged his duties in a satisfactory manner". In the years ahead he would become one of the most influential figures in British sport, and acted as starter at the first *AAC Champion Meeting*, and easily won the 7-Mile

Chambers in later life

Walk. After he graduated in May 1865, he secured an editorial job at *Land and Water*, a relatively new sporting magazine aimed at country gentlemen, which was to prove an important vehicle to promote the AAC.

He had always had big ideas, and now he had the vehicle to express them, and six weeks before the first *AAC Champion Meeting* in he wrote in *Land and Water* of the importance of the AAC. Firstly, there was the need, he wrote, for a "Championship Meeting", but this was coupled with the need for a "centre" that would serve for athletics the same function that Newmarket did for horse-racing, and that centre had to be in London.

The grounds at Beaufort House, however, had already become something of a centre for athletics, and they were, of course, in London. In 1864 and 1865, two of the largest and most successful athletics meetings ever held had taken place on the grounds of Beaufort House; they were the *Civil Service Athletics Sports*, and their programme was so large it took up two days and included, 100yds, 440yds, 880yds, 1-Mile, High Jump, Long Jump, Pole Vault, Shot Put, Hammer Throw, Hurdles, and 3-Mile Walk, plus many others that did not survive.

A committee of five organised the first *Civil Service Athletics Sports*, but the driving force was W.G. Herbert, who was the secretary, and Charles Guy Pym; both were from the War Office. With access to people and resources, they appointed Mr Jones, a War Office Surveyor, who laid out the track, etc., and constructed a stand for spectators. The committee members also acted as stewards at the sports, with E. Page (from the Post Office) acting as Starter. They invited Charles Westhall, the famous all-round professional ex-athlete to act as Umpire. But the Civil Service organising committee had not merely put on a successful athletics meeting, nor just created a track specially for it, they provided an impressive array of silver cups, and paid great attention to attracting, and then entertaining, the crowd. Admission was free, but tickets had to be secured in advance, the band of *The Commissionaires* played throughout the two days, and an information board was set up to help the crowd identify the competitors, and to communicate the results as soon as they were known. A carriage park was even provided, and the press were fed with information before and during the event.

In 1865, the committee was expanded to six but the nucleus remained the same, Herbert, Pym, and Page, with Westhall acting as Umpire on the day. They expanded the programme to nineteen events spread over two days, and attracted so many competitors that three of the events required heats, and the Half-Mile alone attracted thirty-three competitors, and the 100yds, thirty-nine! Once again, good prizes had been on offer (silver cups, goblets, silver-plated salvers, etc), and the athletes, the crowd and the press declared it a huge success. On the first day, the newspapers reported that "there could not have been less than 3,000" in the crowd, and another paper wrote that "there could not have been less than 5,000" on the second, and it including Lord, Ladies, at least one Earl, a Viscountess, and a Marchioness.

With such successful sports and an accessible and popular venue, it is hardly surprising that the meeting at the *Charing Cross Hotel* selected Charles Guy Pym, not only as one of the *Committee of Nine*, but as its Secretary. Charles Guy Pym was not just a committee member and administrator, he was an all-round athlete and competed for the Civil Service at Cricket and Football, but above all else, he regarded himself as an athlete. In 1864, at the *Civil Service*

Athletics Sports, he won the Quarter-Mile, 1-Mile, and HJ, and competed in the Broad Jump, and Putting the Stone, and won the Ladies' Prize for winning the greatest number of events. In 1865, he won the 250yds, Quarter-Mile, and Half-Mile, and competed in the 100yd too, but his ambition was far greater than that. He thought he was the best in Britain and wanted to prove it, but with no recognised Championship he had to do it the hard way.

In the late summer and autumn of 1865 Pym put himself into training with Jem Howse from Stepney, who was a well-known professional runner who had been running matches from half-a-mile to two miles, for nearly ten years. It was Jem Howse' job to prepare Pym for a series of challenges, each one to a runner who could be considered to be the champion of a major sector of the sport. On a Saturday in late August, the first race came off. Pym had challenged Lieutenant Isherwood to a Half-Mile race for a cup valued at £50 [worth £4,270 in 2016]. Isherwood of the 69th (South Lincolnshire) Light Infantry, was the army champion having won the Half-Mile gold cup at Aldershot. The race was run at Beaufort House, now described as the *Civil Service Race Course*. Pym beat him with ease.

Pym also challenged J.D. Hogarth to a Half-Mile race. Hogarth was 26 and from Liverpool, and had previously won twenty races and held 15 cups and medals for running, swimming and rowing. He trained at *Strawberry Gardens* in Liverpool, and was helping Liverpool establish itself as one of the great northern centre for athletics. It had a successful *Liverpool Athletic Club*, had held four *Olympic Festivals* in four consecutive years (1862-1865), and had opened the *Liverpool Gymnasium*. Hogarth could be considered the champion of the north, and it was claimed that he had run the Half-Mile in 2min 2s. The race took place in early November and was held at Beaufort House. *The Morning Post* speculated whether they were running for a silver cup worth £50, or for "50 a side" but concluded that, either way, Pym could only be considered to be a professional runner from then on. Pym wrote in reply, however, saying he *did* still consider himself to be an amateur, and rebuked the paper for interesting itself in a private matter conducted on private ground! In the race, Pym won again, reportedly, going through the first Quarter-Mile in 52s, easily! In trying to stay with Pym's early pace, Hogarth blew up, and Pym finished as he pleased.

Pym sent his third challenge to Cambridge University for them to nominate an athlete to run a Quarter-Mile against him for a gold cup, but because of the fuss made about the prize the week before, Pym told the press that the race was for "a piece of plate". He must have approached Cambridge because they were the current *Inter-Varsity Athletics* champions (they had won 6-3 against Oxford in April) and because they had the winning 440yds runner there at Trinity College. They selected Percy Thornton who had been the Cambridge University *victor ludorum* in 1862 and 1863, and so this was the Universities' champion against the Civil Services' champion, and they were described as "probably the two fastest pedestrians of the present day".

It created enormous interest and as 3 o'clock approached, Beaufort House was "much crowded with civil servants of the Crown, and members and members of the two Universities of Oxford and Cambridge"; *Bell's Life* went further, and wrote that "most of the expected competitors at the forthcoming inter Varsity matches" had travelled there to see them. Once the match had been arranged, Thornton went to Brompton to train under E. Jones, but after Pym's success the previous week, Pym was 2 to 1 favourite.

The day was organised with a theatrical eye by Pym; each of the runners was escorted to the start, Pym by the 19-year-old Lord Arthur Hill, and Thornton by Richard Webster (the Inter-Varsity 1-Mile and 2-Mile winner). Jem Howes and E. Jones accompanied them as their respective bottle-holders as if it was to be a prize fight. Waiting at the starting line was the starter, Lt. F. Young of the 2nd Life Guards, and Charles Westhall, the referee, who asked the athletes to strip for action, and then tossed a coin to decide position. Thornton won and took the inside, and it seems that they ran clockwise around the track.

At the start, Guy Pym got a flier and was called back, but they got off fairly at the second attempt, and they ran together to the first turn. Pym ran a little wide going into the turn which enabled him to get half a yard advantage, and settled into a good fast rhythm past the rifle butts, and going into the second turn at 300yds was able to take the inside position. He rushed into the home straight with a lead of a yard and a half, but with Thornton chasing hard and closing, but it was his final effort. Pym struck again and went away, eventually winning by 8 yards. This was an old-style head-to-head match such as the professional peds took part in, in which official timekeepers were unnecessary. *The Sporting Life*, however, reported that the time was "rather less than 51 seconds". *Bell's Life* gave the time as 50¼s, but Thornton believed it was *under* 50s, and *Bell's Weekly Messenger*, *The Morning Post* and *The Standard* agreed, giving the time as 49 7/10s, - the fastest time by an amateur ever, but, *any* of those times would have given him that distinction, and that, despite the track being described by Thornton as "heavy and not comparable to those at the Universities". In the first *AAC Champion Meeting*, Thornton won the Half-Mile easily in 2m 7s. - Pym did not enter, he had entered the Quarter-Mile but could not take part.

Nevertheless, in the autumn of 1865, Charles Guy Pym had beaten the best from the army, the best from the universities, and the best from the North, and was already the Civil Service Champion; if he couldn't call himself British Champion he had gone as close as he could, and if he didn't call the meeting five weeks later, at the *Charing Cross Hotel*, he would have been delighted that someone had. With the formation of the AAC there could be properly recognised Champions across all athletics' disciplines, and anyone could enter; they would have to be amateurs, of course, - so a definition was needed. Entry to the first AAC *Champion Meeting* was restricted to anyone "who has never entered any open race or handicap with professionals, or for public or gate money".

A.A.C. Prospectus

The AAC Committee was enormously ambitious, and put out a Prospectus that outlined their objectives, eligibility for membership, and subscriptions. Their first objective was to have their own ground free from professionals, and it was to put on an *Annual Prize Champion Meeting* open to all "Gentleman Amateurs", plus other, "open" meetings.

The AAC was to be a private club, with membership open only to officers of the army and navy on full pay, members of the civil service, the universities [then only Oxford, Cambridge,

London, Durham, St. Andrews, Glasgow, Aberdeen, Edinburgh, and the Queen's University, Belfast], the Bar, and the principal "London Clubs". Anyone else had to go through a ballot process. Members would get admission to the AAC's ground, gymnasium, and Racquet Courts (which they did not yet have). They also had visions of a Club House and Swimming Bath. But behind their ambitious plans there was another clear stimulus - if they didn't organise things quickly, someone else would. Membership was 3 guineas [worth £260 in 2016] for *Residents* (i.e. Londoners), and one guinea of *Country* members. But Membership of the AAC and entry to the *AAC Champion Meeting* were entirely independent of each other; many AAC members entered the Champion Meeting, but all represented another club, not the AAC, for the AAC wasn't a club like other clubs, it was to be the new sport's Governing Body.

Future Championships

So successful was the 1866 Champion Meeting that the AAC arranged similar meetings in each of the following years -

1866	Friday 23 March	Beaufort House, Walham Green, Fulham, London
1867	Monday 15 April	Beaufort House, Walham Green, Fulham, London
1868	Fri/Sat 19/20 June	Beaufort House, Walham Green, Fulham, London
1869	Saturday 3 April	Lillie Bridge, West Brompton, London
1870	Fri/Sat 8/9 April	Lillie Bridge, West Brompton, London
1871	Monday 3 April	Lillie Bridge, West Brompton, London
1872	Wednesday 27 March	Lillie Bridge, West Brompton, London
1873	Saturday 5 April	Lillie Bridge, West Brompton, London
1874	Monday 30 March	Lillie Bridge, West Brompton, London
1875	Monday 22 March	Lillie Bridge, West Brompton, London
1876	Monday 10 April	Lillie Bridge, West Brompton, London
1877	Monday 26 March	Lillie Bridge, West Brompton, London
1878	Monday 15 April	Lillie Bridge, West Brompton, London
1879	Monday 7 April	Lillie Bridge, West Brompton, London

In 1880 the AAA took over the Championships and their history is to be found in *The Official History of the AAA*, by Peter Lovesey (1979), and *The Official History of the AAA 1880-2010*, by Mel Watman (2011).

Sources

Where possible, contemporary sources and eye-witness accounts have been used, among which the following have been particularly useful.

Books
Walter Pilkington, *The Athlete for 1866* (London: Chapman and Hall, 1867).
Percy M. Thornton, *Some Things We Have Remembered* (London: Longman's, Green & Co., 1912).
Henry F. Wilkinson, *Modern Athletics* (London: Frederick Warne and Company, 1868).

Newspapers
Bell's Life in London and Sporting Chronicle
Cambridge Chronicle and University Journal
The Chelmsford Chronicle
The Daily News
The Evening Standard
Evening Mail
The Express (Dublin)
The Inverness Courier and General Advertiser
The Illustrated London News
Illustrated Times
Land and Water
The Morning Advertiser
The Morning Post
The Penny Illustrated Paper
The Sportsman
The Sporting Life
The West London Observer
The West Middlesex Advertiser

Other
Amateur Athletic Association, *The Report of The Coming of Age Dinner, June 8th 1901*, (London: The Amateur Athletic Association, 1901).
Amateur Athletic Club, *Prospectus*, undated (December, 1865?).
Amateur Athletic Club, *Champion Meeting, Programme*, Friday 23 March 1866.
The Sporting Mirror, Volume V (January-June 1883).
www.measuringworth.com/ppoweruk (purchasing power of British Pounds)

Illustrations
Illustrations 1-8 are from the author's collection. The portrait of J.G. Chambers is by courtesy of Peter Lovesey.

Further reading

If you have found this account of the 1866 AAC Champion Meeting interesting, and would like to read more, digital, on-line copies of the athletics literature leading up to, and following 1866, are to be found at no cost on http://www.athlos.co.uk.

Anyone interested in this period of athletics history should consult the ultimate source of athletes, and their performances, etc:

Peter Lovesey and Keith Morbey, *British Athletics 1866-80* (https://www.lulu.com) 2016.